Profiles of Integrity

3

Real People Who Demonstrated Godly Character

Marilyn Boyer &
Grace Tumas Ehrman

Master Books First Printing: January 2026

Master Books, P.O. Box 726, Green Forest, AR 72638

Master Books® is a division of
the New Leaf Publishing Group, LLC.

ISBN: 978-1-68344-431-2
ISBN: 978-1-61458-950-1 (digital)

All Scripture verses are from the King James Version of the Bible.

Please consider requesting that a copy of this volume be purchased by your local library system.

Printed in the United States of America

Please visit our website for other great titles:
www.masterbooks.com

For information regarding promotional opportunities, please contact the publicity department at pr@nlpg.com.

Profiles of Integrity

3

*Real People
Who Demonstrated
Godly Character*

Marilyn Boyer &
Grace Tumas Ehrman

Credits

Thanks to the following people for their indispensable help in writing *Portraits of Integrity*:

Grace Tumas Ehrman, for her sensitive and colorful portrayal of these heroes in writing their stories.

Mary Ann Edman who, with help from her husband Ed, produced the layout and design, along with other beautiful graphic effects. Thanks, Mary Ann, for your commitment to excellence!

And Judy Saunders, Krystyn Walker, and Grace Boyer for their proofreading work.

Chronological Table of Contents

Introduction 9

Booker T. Washington ~ Thoroughness
1872 13

Horatio Spafford ~ Contentment
November 1873 19

Kate Gibson ~ Hospitality
Christmas 1875 27

Kate Shelley ~ Self-Control
July 1881 41

George Washington Carver ~ Meekness
1896 49

Lieutenant Armand Pinsard ~ Joyfulness
February 1915 59

Colonel Aleksandr Groten ~ Courage
Autumn 1915 67

Darya Efimova ~ Loyalty
December 1917 75

Sergeant Alvin C. York ~ Obedience
October 1918 91

Gregory Burmistr ~ Compassion
March 1919 105

Selected Bibliography 111
Image Credits 118
About the Authors 121

Table of Contents by Character Quality

Compassion ~ Gregory Burmistr 104
Contentment ~ Horatio Spafford 18
Courage ~ Colonel Aleksandr Groten 66
Hospitality ~ Kate Gibson 26
Joyfulness ~ Lieutenant Armand Pinsard 58
Loyalty ~ Darya Efimova 74
Meekness ~ George Washington Carver 48
Obedience ~ Sergeant Alvin C. York 90
Self-Control ~ Kate Shelley 40
Thoroughness ~ Booker T. Washington 12

Introduction

Prepare to be inspired by amazing men and women who left us a legacy of character to emulate. Both Booker T. Washington and George Washington Carver had a seemingly impossible start to life and yet they served God and left us a shining example to be followed today.

Horatio Spafford lost his daughters to a storm, yet he trusted God's goodness and left us with the hymn 'It is Well with My Soul' which has blessed countless generations. Kate Shelley risked her life to save multiple passengers on a doomed train. Lieutenant Armand Pinsard managed to maintain a joyful attitude in impossible circumstances and finally dig his way out to freedom and an Allied victory.

Alvin York was saved miraculously, stood strong for his beliefs and ended up as a war hero.

We trust in a loving Savior who has the universe under control and works all things together for our good. May you learn to trust and love Him more as a result of reading these stories.

Marilyn Boyer

Character is power.

Character, not circumstances, makes the man.

—Booker T. Washington

Thoroughness

DEFINITION

Bringing to completion each task
I do with excellence

MEMORY VERSE

Better is the end of a thing
than the beginning thereof:
and the patient in spirit is better
than the proud in spirit.

Ecclesiastes 7:8

The Broom Test

Booker T. Washington

Hampton Institute, Virginia

1872

"Ma'am?"

His voice had a soft Virginia drawl. Miss Mary F. Mackie, the headmistress at Hampton Institute, glanced sharply over her desk at him.

"Just how much money do you have?"

"Fifty cents."

Hampton board was ten dollars a month, tuition another $70 per year. She pursed her lips and shook her head.

"Next!"

Sixteen-year-old Booker T. Washington's grubby brown face fell. She wouldn't take him. She actually wouldn't take him. After all those years working for Mrs. Viola Ruffner, scraping pennies together, they weren't even going to let him in. Maybe it was his clothes. He glanced at his filthy jacket, his muddy homespun jeans. He hadn't had a bath in months.

Tall Black men in second-hand suits pushed past him, books tucked under their arms. Girls with cotton dresses and black hair twisted into chignons signed in at the desk. They all trooped by him, a strong and proud race, and disappeared into classrooms he couldn't see. He could hear them talking, laughing. So this was Hampton Institute, built in 1868 by its hero, General Samuel Chapman Armstrong. It had smooth green lawns, the large red-brick building with its steep slate roof stretching like a castle to the sky. The place he had dreamed about back in the little log cabin in Malden, West Virginia. The place he had walked over 500 miles to attend. Sleeping under wooden sidewalks, slaving on the wharves, begging rides, he trudged the last 80 miles on foot. Now he was penniless. And they wouldn't let him in.

Miss Mackie kept her face turned away from him, ignoring him. She looked hard as flint.

A Yankee woman. If only he had a chance to prove that he was worth something! Ever since he had sweated in the coal mines of West Virginia, teaching himself to read from letters stamped on the barrels, he had dreamed of this day. In Hampton classrooms students learned mysterious numbers, words that made your heart beat, lands and oceans, whole planets of knowledge. Books lined the shelves. He ached to know what was in them. To take them down and touch their pages.

Booker T. Washington

The last students had gone. His legs hurt from standing so long. But he wouldn't leave.

Suddenly, Miss Mackie spoke. "The recitation room needs sweeping. Take the broom and sweep it."

This was his chance. Now he could prove to her that he was good enough to stay. Grimy floors, chalkboards covered with white dust greeted him as he entered the schoolroom. He set to work. He swept the floor three times. Then he wet a dust cloth and carefully rubbed down each bench, table, and desk. He climbed up to reach and dust the woodwork. He wiped the walls and the baseboards near the floor. He dragged every piece of furniture out of its place, cleaned under it, and pushed it back again. He opened doors and cleaned out all the closets. He even poked his dust rag into corners until the room shone. When he had dusted the whole place thoroughly, he did it a second time. And a third. After the fourth time around, he stepped back, satisfied. The President of the United States could want it no cleaner. How glad he was that that stern Yankee woman, Mrs. Ruffner, had taught him such thoroughness! Now he couldn't enter a room without picking up a scrap of paper or running his sleeve across a dusty chair. He called Miss Mackie.

She swept into the room. His heart pounded as he watched her. She knew just where to look for dust. Bending down, she swiped her clean white handkerchief across the undersides of the benches. She peered into closets, ran her hand over the woodwork, the tables and desks. She inspected the floor. Finally, she stood up and looked at him. Her handkerchief had not picked up one speck of dirt or a particle of dust from any surface in the room. It was absolutely clean.

When she spoke, her voice was quiet. "I guess you will do to enter this school."

He had passed his college test with flying colors. He would work hard, pay off his tuition. At last he had proved himself worthy of Hampton Institute.

Because he practiced thoroughness in his life, Booker T. Washington could perform a difficult task given to him. His thoroughness not only enabled him to enter college, but paved the way for a long life of usefulness to his fellow Americans as president of Tuskegee Institute.

Questions

1. How far had Booker T. Washington walked to get to Hampton University?
2. How had he earned the money to travel there?
3. Why did they initially turn him down?
4. Why did he want to attend school?
5. What test did Mrs. Mackie give to him? What was her purpose in doing so?
6. How did he perform the job?
7. How had he learned the skill of thoroughness which prepared him to pass this unusual test?
8. How had Booker's mastering the quality of thoroughness been used to impact the lives of many?
9. Isn't it amazing how God prepares people for future effectiveness through simple disciplines in the early years of their lives? Think of some opportunities you have right now to cultivate thoroughness in your life.

Contentment

DEFINITION

Realizing that God has given me all I need for my present happiness

MEMORY VERSE

Not that I speak in respect of want: for I have learned, in whatsoever state I am, therewith to be content. I know how to be abased, and I know how to abound: everywhere and in all things I am instructed both to be full and to be hungry, both to abound and to suffer need.

Philippians 4:11-12

Waterland

Horatio Spafford

The Atlantic Ocean

November, 1873

November 22, 1873. The passenger steamer, *Ville du Havre*, sailing from the United States to Europe, cut through the frigid autumn waters and sea mists around the rocky coastline of Newfoundland at a steady clip. Within its lighted decks and third-class berths it carried 107 people. Suddenly, a heavy vessel flying the red-blue-and-white British flag loomed up out of the fog like an iron monster. Too late to turn, the *Loch Earn* struck the *Ville* with a grinding crunch. Inside, tables lurched and chairs overturned. People

Horatio Spafford

ran towards the lifeboats as water began gushing into the ship's hold. In twelve minutes, the deck began tilting upwards before diving straight down towards the bottom of the sea. Within twenty minutes, it disappeared completely.

Anna Spafford surfaced amid choppy waves and bits of refuse. Suddenly, a swirling vortex sucked her head underwater. Her baby was torn from her arms. Surfacing again, the waves smashed her body against a pile of debris, bruising her arms. Just then, she saw the baby's dress sinking through the water. She flailed out desperately, clutching at the soggy clothing. Her fingers closed on the seams. Then another wave knocked her away and the baby sank like a stone. Out to sea, a young man riding a chunk of wood grabbed the two girls, Annie and Maggie, and told them to hang onto his coat pockets as he searched for a larger piece of wreckage. Thirty minutes later, he seized a plank drifting by. Struggling to pull the girls aboard, he saw their eyes close and their fingers slip away. Then they were gone. Nobody saw the fourth child.

Gasping and shivering, her hair shimmering with salt and her dressing gown hanging in tatters from her shoulders, Anna clung with both hands to a piece of floating wreckage, bobbing like a cork alone in the pitiless "waterland" of an endless sea. All she could hear in her pain-numbed mind were the words, "You were saved for a purpose!

Anna Spafford

Someday, God, I will know why this happened. But not now."

Back home, the air still smelled like fire. Sometimes it crept out of odd corners, through the sweet-smelling yellow timbers, fresh mortar and new red bricks going up all over the city. The skyline of Chicago had changed. Gone were the rickety old tenement houses, the tumbledown stables full of musty hay, the wealthy houses lining the waterfront near Lake Michigan. When the Great Fire of October, 1871, killed 300 people and left another 100,000 homeless, Horatio G. Spafford had lost almost everything to the flames.

Alone in his house in the northern suburbs, he was busy clearing up some urgent law business before leaving for Europe to meet his wife and daughters.

The house was quiet now. No sounds of girlish laughter from eleven-year-old Annie, nine-year-old Maggie, five-year-old Bessie and baby Tanetta. Together, he and Anna, his soft-faced Swedish wife, welcomed reformers and preachers into their home. But Anna's health had started to crack. To help her recover, the Spaffords planned a trip to Europe in the autumn. They also wanted to assist D. L. Moody and Ira D. Sankey during their popular revivals in England. When sudden business kept him a little longer in Chicago, Spafford sent Anna ahead with the girls.

He waved the girls on board, together with their French governess, Emma Lorriaux. He was confident after a few days, he would see them again. As he cleared up the papers and prepared to leave, a telegraph messenger thrust a paper into his hand. It was from Anna. He tore it open.

The words nearly blinded him. It was Anna screaming at him from across the sea.

"Saved alone. What shall I do?"

He had felt this way before, numb, stunned. When their four-year-old son Horatio slipped into a scarlet-fever coma three years ago, he had felt like dying, too. Now as he stood on the deck of the ship sailing across the Atlantic, to reunite with Anna, he heard the captain's voice calling him up to the bridge.

"A careful reckoning has been made and I believe we are now passing the place where the *Ville du Havre* was wrecked." The captain pointed. "The water is three miles deep."

Three miles deep. He down stared at the slate-grey water. Somewhere down there his beautiful girls lay in a watery grave. Only 47 out of 300 people survived. But not one of his girls. Somehow, although he could not understand it, God had allowed this to happen. Slowly, he turned away from the railing. Sitting alone in his cabin that night, wondering what he would say to Anna when he saw her again, he began to write.

"When peace like a river attendeth my way, when sorrows like sea billows roll, whatever my lot, Thou hast taught me to say, 'It is well, it is well with my soul.' "

Later, Philip Bliss set his words to music. In 1880, Horatio and Anna Spafford settled with their next three children at the "American Colony" in Jerusalem. He and his wife would labor for a Christian utopian community in the land of Israel for the rest of their lives.

Horatio and Anna Spafford demonstrated contentment by accepting through faith the difficult circumstances that God brought into their lives.

When peace like a river, attends my way,
When sorrows like sea billows roll;
Whatever my lot, You have taught me to know
It is well, it is well, with my soul.

It is well, (it is well),
With my soul, (with my soul)
It is well, it is well, with my soul.

—Original lyrics of "It Is Well with My Soul" by Horatio Spafford

Questions

1. What disaster struck the *Ville du Havre?*
2. What happened to Horatio's family?
3. Tell about how the Chicago fire affected the Spafford family earlier.
4. Why did Horatio send his family on ahead to England?
5. Where was Horatio Spafford when he wrote the words to "It Is Well with My Soul?" What motivated him to write them?
6. How did the Spaffords illustrate contentment?
7. How can you comfort and encourage someone who is going through rough circumstances?
8. How might you respond to someone who says God isn't in control of their circumstances?
9. Think of a situation you struggle with. How can you purpose to demonstrate contentment? Remember God has the big picture and He has our best interests in mind. Maybe on earth, but for sure when we get to heaven, we will understand it all, but for now we can trust that God will do what is best for us.

Hospitality

DEFINITION

Making those who visit our home feel comfortable

MEMORY VERSE

. . . Given to hospitality.

Romans 12:13b

The Gift

Kate Gibson

Fort Abraham Lincoln, the Dakota
Christmas, 1875

Christmas Eve brought bright sunshine and six feet of sand-dry snow. Beyond the stockade, the Dakota plains swept east and west to the low, unbroken chain of hills bounding the right bank of the Missouri River outside Fort Rice. Officers of the 7th Cavalry, back from hard-riding patrols, moved about the snow blanketed parade ground, their lean cheeks covered with unshaven stubble. The harsh temperatures, soaring to 110 degrees in the summer months—aggravated by razor-sharp buffalo grass, black flies, and stinging alkali dust—dropped to well below zero in December. An area of 864 feet by 544 feet surrounded by a ten-foot-high log stockade served as a prison, penning 235 men within the stifling confines of barracks, post kitchen, stables, trade store, and guardhouse.

Ice frosted the windows of the low clapboard headquarters building. Kate Gibson turned to survey the room, her blonde hair shining in the light from the window. It was hard to keep this place warm. Homemade adobe bricks, stacked between the rickety wall studs, helped insulate from drafts. But the cold still did its best to penetrate the sawn cottonwood walls.

The door blew open. Lt. Frank Gibson stumbled in, pushing two soldiers with armfuls of squatty sage and cedar brush. He grinned at her, teeth flashing under his dark mustache.

Dear Frank. This was their first Christmas.

Helplessly, she inspected the prickly scrub. She thought of the big, soft green pines glowing with wax candles she had known in the South. There were no trees out here. Only the occasional lonely cottonwood, its bark grey and shaggy as an elephant hide, its silver leaves gone. She looked into Frank's eager face. Well, this would have to do. They must have a tree for Christmas.

Bunching and tying them together, she propped the branches into a kind of tree. Annie Yates and Mrs.

Moylan climbed up on benches to hang greenery in rows from the ceiling. Feathery brushes of cedar almost swept the floor. Kate pushed a washtub covered with brightly painted paper underneath, poured sand into the tub and crammed it with simple gifts brought in on horseback from the town of Bismarck.

Fort Abraham Lincoln officers, 1875

She thought of them all—little Benny Hodgson, who had met her first, Lieutenant Van Riley and his gentle teasing, the half-French scout Mitch Boyer, Tom Custer, who taught her how to ride. By opening her home to them, she wanted to do something to make this Christmas a happy one. To blot out for a few hours burning villages, raids into the Black Hills and hostile parties of the Comanche and Lakota tribes.

The hours before dark went quickly. Yards and yards of paper cut into strips festooned the ceiling. Paper twisted into cornucopias burst with homemade candy. Nuts appeared out of nowhere. Kate tore the silver wrappings off carefully-hoarded cigars. Her slim fingers wrapped and pinched and covered the nuts with foil. Officers, ducking shyly into the room at rare intervals, offered ancient Christmas cards, bits of home life they had lovingly treasured, some from as far back as 1868. Bow-tied with faded scraps of ribbon, they swung on the scraggly branches like stars. Firelight winked on the beads of silver nuts.

Shadows began to fall, lengthening across the parade ground. It was warm inside the Gibsons' headquarters. Stoves crackled with smoking cedar and cottonwood branches, green sap hissing as it dripped onto the flames. Soon guests began to arrive, crowding the room with their tight-fitting, dark-blue uniform coats, boots and rattling sabers. The tree glowed like a friendly spirit, while crimson candles perched jauntily on the branches. Sandwiches, cake, candy, and ersatz lemonade disappeared under laughing mustaches. Some ducked under the big red paper bell floating overhead.

It was impossible to keep her eyes off her husband. He moved easily among the men, tasting the ice cream frugally whipped up with condensed milk, whisked gelatin, and precious egg whites smuggled in beneath the mail courier's buckskin shirt. Frank's saber knocked against his long, blue pants legs as he moved. He had removed the chinstrap of his tall campaign hat with the sleek brown horsetail dangling behind, and his thick dark hair swept his forehead. Thank God, she whispered. Thank God. She hadn't lost him to frostbite or typhoid fever. He hadn't fallen somewhere among the dusty buffalo grass with an arrow in his chest. He was here. He was safe. For another day.

Someone struck up the "Virginia Reel." Stamping their feet, swinging their partners, the officers plunged in, sashaying across the room to the plink-plunk of an ancient banjo, the rhythmic strumming of a guitar, the metallic wheeze of a jaw harp. Clasped hands and sweating faces swayed in the light of the red Christmas candles.

Midnight struck.

Kate saw Frank wish everyone goodnight before slipping out into the cold entry. As Officer of the Day, he had to make his rounds of the stockade that night, checking up on security, questioning the guards who watched the plains for a puff of smoke, the silent flight of an arrow, the distant thundering hooves of a war party raiding cattle and killing traders. She helped him throw the cape over his shoulders, tugging the strap under his chin and pulling on his gloves. His gold epaulettes gleamed faintly as she opened the door for him.

Up on the outposts, the sentries braced their backs against the wind so as not to be blown off. The temperature had dropped again, and the wind brought with it a few big flakes of snow.

The party was almost over. Officers clustered around the table, drinking up the last of the lemonade before putting on their coats and going off to their bachelor quarters.

Goodnight, Merry Christmas.

They were gone at last. Giving one last glance around the room, at the paper garlands and the candles melting down, puddling, Kate moved towards the kitchen. She held the candle high, yellow flickers chasing the shadows down the walls. She opened the door, shivering at the cold blast of air. Where was Frank? She pictured him striding through the silent stockade, footsteps crunching in the snow. The candle flame stabbed the darkness. And she gasped.

Huddled in the side shanty were four or five little figures.

Native American children.

One was barely tall enough to peek in the window. What did they want? Then she saw the tree gleaming dazzlingly through the window, like something out of a magical fairyland. She wondered how they had managed to slip into Fort Rice past the sentries. Then she remembered a slight gap in the stockade wall, just big enough to let a child slip through. It was bitterly cold. She thought "I don't want to frighten them. They're just children." Softly, she opened the door and stood aside.

"Come in."

The tall boy stared at her, supple and straight as a willow wand. She could see fear struggle with yearning in his eyes. Then he stepped forward, grasping the hand of a four-year-old girl. The others followed in single file. She wondered how they had known about the Christmas party going on in the officer's headquarters.

The tree sparkled through the open living room door. "Someone tell you about it?" She spoke slowly, carefully, so that he could grasp the words.

He nodded jerkily.

"Who tell you?"

The answer was quick. "Horn Toad."

"Oh." So that was it. The friendly, good-natured Native American scout loved children, inside the stockade or outside of it.

The little group pressed up against the hot stove, thawing out and staring at her. Nobody moved. Nobody said anything else. She bent down to the little girl.

"And who is she?"

"Sister." The boy spoke abruptly.

Kate stared down into big black eyes. A chubby little hand clung tightly to the boy's. She shivered, clutching an old piece of gunny sack over the shoulders of her thin calico dress. She wore little buckskin leggings and tiny beaded moccasins. A rawhide strip kept back her tangled dark hair. Kate shook herself. This was a terrible hour for these children to be up. She thought of their mothers. They must go back at once.

Then she looked at their shy, eager faces. They must have spent hours out in the cold night, pressing their faces to the window for a glimpse of this glittering paradise. Never mind the time. Their mothers could worry for an hour longer. Closing the door, she shooed them into the living room. There stood the Christmas pie and the washtub that had held the officers' gifts. Digging into the sand, she came up with a Jack-in-the-box. She wrapped the little girl's hands around it. Her black eyes jumped with joy. Hands trembling, she clutched the toy to her chest. Now all the children crowded round the tub, digging busily in the sand.

Kate got up and ran into the kitchen. There was still some hot cocoa left. She was heating it up on the cook-stove when she noticed the sentry was leaving. Suddenly, she pictured Native American women in tattered calico and gunnysack headbands standing forlornly outside the fort, waiting for their children. Perhaps a Native American father with warm buffalo robes and a copper armband. It was best to avoid worry and trouble.

"Oh, Alkorn," she called out, "go to the nearest bastion and tell the sentinel to relay to other sentinels that, in the event of any Native Americans hanging around and looking for children, they are at Lieutenant Gibson's quarters and will be along soon."

Carrying a pot of steaming hot cocoa, she went back to the living room. The children were pawing through the tub, shyness forgotten. There were shrieks of joy as rag dolls and toy pistols came to light. At first, they would not look at the food. Even cocoa held no such magic as these toys. But at last they came to the table. Cradling the cups in their hands, they drank eagerly. Soon color flooded their pinched cheeks and the chilled little fingers grew warm. The children should go home now. But somehow she couldn't send them away. While they sat at the table, she heaped their laps with goodies, candy, popcorn and nuts. There was some ice cream left, too. She couldn't let them go without feeding them. The children stared at the whipped pink-and-white stuff. It was cold. Fluffy. Then the little girl dipped her finger in and licked it. A soft smile spread over her face. All at once, the boys attacked it, stuffing themselves till they ached.

Smacking sounds followed her as she ran upstairs. There must be some old clothes around here somewhere. Blankets, stockings, socks. It was unbearable to think of the little ones going out, facing the cold again with uncovered faces and blue fingers. There—one of her short coats, a couple pairs of mittens, some warm mufflers. Suddenly, she stopped on the stairs, alert, listening. There was a clapping of hands and a weird chanting, soft and first, then louder, more insistent. Then came the shuffle of moccasins. Whoops pierced the air. Sinking down on the steps, she peered through the lower banisters. Her eyes froze.

The oldest boy was the chief. One boy and the little girl stood off to one side, clapping loudly. She swayed her hips and body in time to the music, imitating the older women in a dance of sunflower seeds and deer. Their lips moved in a monotonous chant. There was no tune. Behind them came the young boys, circling the red-hot stove, stamping, shuffling. Their dance was the trampling of buffaloes in the tall grass, it was the fierce lightness of the wildcat, it was the grass itself, swaying, bending, flowing effortlessly. She sat frozen, watching them. Their necks tipped back; eerie whoops burst forth. The candles trembled. Sand was ground into the carpet. But she saw only the graceful young bodies swaying like reeds in the wind. It was a peace dance, a dance of greatness and thanksgiving.

The dance changed. Now it was fast, choppy. The clapping and chanting grew faster. The children whirled, leaping, whooping. The floor shook with their thunder. Then suddenly it all was all over. The young chief held up his hand. The children dropped down, exhausted, on the carpet. Picking up the bunch of winter clothes, Kate hurried downstairs. In the entryway, she bundled the little girl up tight, tied the too-big mittens onto her hands. The scarves, blankets and boots she handed out to the boys and helped them struggle into them. Then she went to the tree, stripped off all the colored gifts and silver nuts, slipped the rest of the cake and candy into a bag, and gave it to the tall boy.

It was hard to let them go. She felt as if they belonged to her. Yet they were part of a way of life

Native American child

she knew little about. The evening spun before her, the officers' boyish faces, their shining eyes, their jokes; and these gentle little strangers, thanking her in the only way they knew how. Tomorrow, these same officers might ride out to face a storm of arrows and carbine bullets from the children's fathers and brothers. Snow crunched crisply as the little group marched single-file across the parade ground. Stars winked above the log palisades. As she stood watching, one by one, the children, clutching their toys, turned for one last look. A last smile. Then the boy bringing up the rear patted his mouth with a slim brown hand, sending the farewell call of his people into the night. In the hall, the clock struck one.

Kate Gibson wearily closed the door. Blowing out the kerosene lamp, she trudged upstairs to bed. Frank would be home at dawn. Outside, the snow drifted down and the sentinels' hollow cry passed from post to post: "One o'clock and all's well." It was Christmas Day, 1875.

By welcoming the curious children into her home, Kate Gibson demonstrated that hospitality should not only be shown to friends and people we want to invite, but to strangers needing food, comfort or love.

I am and always have been a friend of the [Native American]. I have always sympathized with him in his struggle to hold the country that was his by right of birth.

—William F. Cody
(Buffalo Bill)

Questions

1. How did Kate use the quality of hospitality to extend warmth and kindness to others?
2. Whom did she invite for a Christmas celebration?
3. What did she use for a "tree"?
4. How did Kate improvise to make a memorable celebration for the men?
5. Who were the surprise visitors?
6. How did Kate extend hospitality to the children? What was their response?
7. To whom might you extend hospitality? Think of someone who would be blessed by your effort and plan to surprise them.
8. Remember, being hospitable to others is not always convenient for us, but God will bless our efforts. How do you think Kate felt as she wearily made her way to bed after the children left?

Self-Control

DEFINITION

Subjecting my own desire to
the control of the Holy Spirit

MEMORY VERSE

He that hath no rule over his own spirit
is like a city that is broken down
and without walls.
Proverbs 25:28

Midnight Express

Kate Shelley

Honey Creek, Moingona, Iowa

July, 1881

Moingona, Iowa: July 6, 1881. Honey Creek was running high tonight. Flashes of lightning split the sky, and in the flickering white glare the neck of the Des Moines River came into sight, swollen, brown and muddy. Fifteen-year-old Kate Shelley, glancing out the window of the frame house, saw the water rising steadily toward the stable farther down the slope. Throwing a cloak over her head, she slopped through the mud toward the barn. In the warm interior, fragrant with hay and animal smells, she could hear the storm buffeting and raging outside. She had to get the animals out of here. She levered open the door, rain lashing her face, and slapped a cow's rump, sending the unwilling animal galloping out into the rain. Not penned up, the animals would seek the high ground behind the house.

Kate Shelley

Through the sheets of rain, Kate could barely make out the lonely railroad trestle bridging the gap over Honey Creek. Pa would have been out tonight—if the railroad hadn't killed him. Below her, Honey Creek continued to rise. It was no longer the lazy swimming hole that the boys jumped into on summer days. It was suddenly churning, sucking chunks of wood or a terrified cow into its whirlpool. As it had taken Michael, her oldest brother, the summer she turned twelve.

Inside the house, she and her mother watched as the water level continued to rise. Night came on and they still sat up, waiting and listening. Suddenly, at eleven o'clock, Kate heard another sound over the roar of the rain. It was a pusher locomotive, No. 12, crossing the Des Moines River Bridge a short distance away. With four men, Ed Wood, George Olmstead, Adam Agar and Patrick Donahue aboard, it rumbled towards the Honey Creek crossing.

Despite the storm, they had to check the track conditions and make it back to Moingona that night.

Kate heard the bell ring twice, warningly. Then she heard a horrible crash and a fierce hiss of steam as the engine plunged through the bridge into Honey Creek below. Kate sat stunned for a moment. And then a terrible thought flashed into her mind.

Another train was due any minute now. The western express would soon approach the same bridge—and crash. She had to try to cross the long Des Moines River Bridge to stop the train before it reached Honey Creek. Kate grabbed one of her father's railroad lanterns. Dressed in an old coat and skirt, with a straw hat clamped on her head, she ran out into the storm.

Waving her lantern, she stumbled down the bank to the washed-out bridge. Lightning shattered the ground around her. In its glare, she saw Wood and Ager clinging to the branches of a tree. She couldn't see the other two men. Maybe they had washed downstream, swept out into the low-lying cornfield to rot with the grain. She couldn't help them. She could only help the coming express roaring towards Moingona on its way through Boone County. And it wouldn't stop unless she got there in time.

She reached the Moingona Bridge, the little catwalk winding up like the backbone of a lizard in the dark. It was dangerous to cross the high bridge even on a clear day. People sometimes climbed up and walked along the rail, and it was easy to catch an ankle and fall down as a train bore down on them. As Kate started across, she saw that large pieces of the flooring had been torn out, leaving black gaps between the ties. The wind nearly knocked her off her feet. Willow trees struggled to keep their heads above water, fingers desperately gripping the river-bank as roots were being torn from the depths.

She grabbed for a railroad tie and knelt there, panting. She would have to crawl on her hands and knees. She set the lantern down, trying to see in a blur of lashing leaves and rain. The yellow light looked like a pinpoint in the blackness. The roar of the river filled her ears. Michael had drowned here. She didn't look down. Inch by inch, she groped her way along. The wind snatched at her clothes, trying to drag her off the trestle. Wood splinters stabbed her palms. Spikes bruised her hands and tore her skirt. The lantern went out. She felt before her in total darkness, concentrating on the next tie, her hand plunging into empty air over a torn-out span. Half-way, a tree crashed towards the bridge, threatening to snap the trestle in two. Then the tree slipped between the spans and hurtled into the river below. Every second, she expected to see the sudden glare of train lights, hear the deafening whoooo, the thunder of wheels on the tracks. The last thing she would hear.

Suddenly, she put out her hand and touched a railroad tie. Solid ground. She was across. She began

Kate Shelley Bridge

running down the half-mile of track. Wild-eyed, she burst into the station and gasped out her story about the washed-out bridge and the coming express.

Someone exclaimed: "The girl is crazy!"

Then Kate Shelley fainted. As she lay on the floor in her torn coat, her wet hair falling around her face, the station master recognized her. He knew that he had to stop the express. He ran out into the rain, waving a red lantern just as the midnight express bore down on the station with 200 passengers aboard. A few minutes later, Kate woke up. Late that night, Kate led a rescue crew to Honey Creek Bridge, where the men from No. 12 had gone down. Afterwards, the passengers of the midnight express took up a collection of several hundred dollars for her. The State of Iowa presented Kate with a medal. She is the first woman to have a bridge named after her: one spanning the Des Moines River at the point she crossed the night of July 6–7, 1881.

Kate Shelley exhibited self-control by staying calm under difficult circumstances and focusing on one part of her task at a time until she completed it.

Most men who have really lived have had, in some shape, their great adventure. This railway is mine.

—James J. Hill, founder of the Great Northern Railway

Questions

1. How old was Kate Shelley in this story?
2. What did Kate do to rescue the animals?
3. What natural disaster was brewing?
4. What had happened to her brother in the past?
5. What was the horrible sound Kate heard?
6. Another disaster was about to happen. What was it?
7. How did Kate risk her safety to rescue others?
8. Was the train rescued?
9. How did Kate demonstrated self-control?
10. Self-control can be demonstrated in times of crisis and also in day-to-day life. As you strive to learn self-control in little areas, God will grow you so you can respond to crisis situations with self-control. Think of the last time you demonstrated self-control when it was really hard to do so.
11. Think of a situation that happens often that tempts you not to demonstrate self control. Purpose to pursue self-control in your life in little areas. In what areas do you need help with self-control—eating? Kindness to others? Irritations? Temper?

Meekness

DEFINITION

Yielding my expectations (rights)
to God without getting angry

MEMORY VERSE

The meek will he guide in judgment:
and the meek will he teach his way.
Psalm 25:9

The Plant Doctor

George Washington Carver

Tuskegee Institute, Tuskegee, Alabama

1896

He had always loved plants. They vibrated under his fingers like sea anemones, bursting into leaf, fruit, and flower. Pottering around in his laboratory, the tall, distinguished-looking professor felt the leaves quiver as he touched them with the same life that danced in his music or leaped onto the canvas with swift brush-strokes from his painter's pallet. Now, late at night, he hunched over a single yellow lamp. Outside, a student banged on the door.

"Are you all right, Dr. Carver?"

He glanced up, bewildered. "Yes! Yes! Please let me be."

George Washington Carver

Someday, George Washington Carver, born a slave, would produce a product that would benefit poor sharecropping farmers in the exhausted land of the post-war South.

Wearing a baggy hat and a patched sweater, Carver sauntered slowly along the country road. A woman had called at the Institute to see if "the Tuskegee man" would help her withering peach trees. As he drew near, the woman saw a shabby, somber-faced Black man coming across the lawn.

"Do you want to earn fifty cents cutting my grass?" she called out. He remained silent. Going quietly to the mower, he began pushing it back and forth through the long grass. He crisscrossed the front lawn. He mowed the back. Then he went to the door and knocked politely.

When she opened the door, he said softly, "Now, what seems to be the trouble with your peaches, Ma'am?"

He could not remember his mother. In the shadowy nighttime of 1865, a gang of Confederate bushwhackers swooped down on the slave cabins on the Carver farm near Diamond, Missouri. They grabbed his mother, tearing the baby from her arms and forcing her out of the cabin. Farther along the road, they threw him into a ditch and rode off. The next day, a neighbor found the baby and returned him to his owners, Moses and Sarah Carver. Raised as one of their own children, George ran about the farm, collecting rocks, digging up plants, catching frogs and examining insects. When neighbors brought him their dying plants, he took them to his little workshop in the woods and nursed them back to health. He seemed to have a magic touch when it came to the complex natural world around him. Locals called him the "plant doctor."

His mind thirsted for knowledge. But every school shut their doors to him because of his ethnicity. At age fourteen, he learned of a school for Black students in Neosho, Missouri. When he limped into town, he had no money and nowhere to go. As he ambled along the street towards the schoolhouse, a Black woman called out to him from her backyard. Her name was Moriah Watkins, a childless washerwoman. From that evening, he ate and slept at her house, attending classes in the bitterly cold schoolhouse and helping Moriah's husband with odd jobs after hours.

During the next hard years, George Washington Carver finished grade school and high school, and then tried to enter college. Poor, dusty, and exhausted, the tall, handsome young man trudged on foot to Highland College, overjoyed at his letter

Dr. Carver studying plants

of acceptance. When he arrived at the university's office, the president stared at him. "You didn't tell me you were Black," he said accusingly. "Highland College does not take Black people." But Carver did not give up. Finally, in 1890, at the age of thirty, he walked thirty miles to Simpson College in Indianola, Iowa, and was accepted. To support himself, he cooked and sold hominy, and he washed, ironed, and mended his classmates' laundry. He also served as a janitor, waiter, greenhouse worker, and laboratory assistant. No task was too menial, no job too dirty for him to perform gladly. Others noticed the young man's meekness, grace, and dignity. Meanwhile, he studied voraciously: music, art, botany, chemistry, geometry, zoology, and bacteriology.

In 1896, he graduated with a Master's Degree from Iowa State University. Then Booker T. Washington, struggling to keep the flame of Black education alive in Tuskegee, Alabama, wrote him a letter offering Carver the chance to benefit his countrymen through research. "I cannot offer you money, position, or fame," Washington argued. "The first two you have. The last . . . you will no doubt achieve. These things I ask you to give up. I offer you, in their place, work—hard, hard work—the task of bringing a people from degradation, poverty, and waste to full manhood."

Some laboratories offered Carver over $100,000 per year (almost a million dollars today) to work for them. Booker T. Washington could only offer him a pittance of $125 per month.

Feeling that God wanted him to work for Tuskegee, Carver gave up his seat on the faculty at Iowa State University. As the Director of Agriculture at Tuskegee, he showed students that they threw away rich plant food every day. For instance, he pointed out the despised cowpea (also known as the black-eyed pea). Southerners did not even consider the cowpea as food, but rather as cattle fodder. Carver sent his students hiking through the woods to fill their buckets with leaf mold to spread on their gardens. He had discovered that cowpeas actually draw nitrogen from the air and then release it back into the soil.

Carver observed how cotton crops depleted the soil's nutrients without replenishing them. Instead of always planting cotton, he urged farmers to alternate with enriching legumes like soybeans and peanuts, as well as sweet potatoes and pecans. By promoting variable crops, he demonstrated ways to help the land recover from the destruction of the Civil War. This transition from plantations to farms run by former slaves helped the South to regain economic stability.

Years passed. Carver never married. When urged to, the professor smiled gently. "What woman would want a husband forever dropping soil specimens all over her parlor? How could I explain to a wife that I need to go out at 4 a.m. every morning to talk to the flowers?"

Dr. Carver experimenting in his laboratory

He lived in one of the Tuskegee dormitories and walked daily to work in his laboratory. The peanut grew and flourished. Working with fields and test tubes, he discovered three hundred useful products made from peanuts. He made milk, cheese, soap, bleach, axle grease, adhesives, fuel, instant coffee, ink, buttermilk, mayonnaise, chili sauce, meat tenderizer, paper, linoleum, shoe polish, and pavement. As he went on testing, the possibilities seemed endless: Shaving cream, metal polish, talcum powder, synthetic rubber, and wood stain. By varying their crops and improving their diets with simple plants, Carver improved the standard of living for many rural families in the South. No longer would a farmer be dependent on a single market for his produce. Now, he could sell his peanut and soybean crops to industrialists and food manufacturers.

A devout Christian who called his laboratory "God's little workshop," Carver also taught a Bible class every Sunday afternoon. He still drew his original $125 a month. Under his hands, the ordinary peanut oozed milk. It turned into fine dust as a base for cosmetics. It stretched into synthetic rubber. For all of this, Carver took no credit. He refused to take out a patent on more than three inventions, saying, "God gave them to me. How can I sell them to someone else?"

George Washington Carver demonstrated meekness by performing menial tasks with humility and refusing to take the glory for his discoveries for himself.

How far you go in life depends on your being tender to the young, compassionate with the aged, sympathetic with the striving and tolerant of the weak and strong. Because someday in your life you will have been all of these.

—George Washington Carver

Questions

1. What did George Washington Carver delight in studying?
2. How did he demonstrate meekness when the lady mistook him for being a servant?
3. What happened to his mother and father?
4. How did he come to live with the Carvers? Tell how he was treated by the Carvers.
5. How did Moriah Watkins prove a blessing in his life?
6. What college turned him down because of his color?
7. How did he support himself while attending Simpson College?
8. What was Booker T. Washington's offer to Carver?
9. What did Carver accomplish in his time there?
10 What was he able to make from the peanut?
11. How did he help to improve the standard of living for the Southern farmers?
12. What did he call his workshop?
13. How did Carver demonstrate meekness when praised by others?
14. How can you choose to live a life of meekness? When tempted to be angry? When tempted to take credit for yourself?

Joyfulness

DEFINITION

Choosing to have a good attitude even when circumstances are tough to bear

MEMORY VERSE

Rejoice in the Lord always;
and again I say, Rejoice.
Philippians 4:4

Fortress Escape

Lieutenant Armand Pinsard

World War I, Germany

February, 1915

He was the eighth highest-scoring French fighting ace, with twenty-seven "kills" under his belt. The first man to drop an espionage agent behind German lines. He could not know that the story of his escape and his attitude under adversity would inspire the greatest anti-war film of all time.

February 8, 1915. As his plane crashed to the ground, riddled with bullets, Lieutenant Armand Pinsard saw pale-blue trench coats and spiked German helmets running across the field towards him. Then pain engulfed his body, searing it like flames as he spun into oblivion.

Armand Pinsard, staring down the window in his prison quarters, watched German soldiers goose-stepping in the courtyard below. His straight nose and elegant, mustached profile made the French fighter pilot look older than his twenty-eight years. Singlehandedly, Pinsard would shoot down eighteen German bombers and nine observation balloons filled with lethal gas; strafe trains loaded with enemy troops; and halt a deadly German counterattack from the air.

Again he felt his squadron N26 plane forced down behind German lines. The grinding crash. The dark weeks of pain. After a month, the pain began to subside. He could get out of bed, walk to the window and back. Now he could think of escape. Behind him, the other officers crouched on their beds, playing cards and chaffing at their imprisonment. Technically, the Germans could not force officers to do hard labor. Compared to the soldiers who slogged it out in muddy camps at Soldau or Oberhofen, this was paradise. But it was also an illusion. While treated with greater dignity, he knew it was easier for soldiers to escape while on work detail into the nearby woods or fields. Camp regulations forbade officers to wear or receive civilian clothes. This made the chance of escaping and blending in with the German countryside virtually impossible.

From where he stood, Pinsard could see, like succeeding rings of frost, the solid barracks wall, the motionless statues of the guards, and beyond that the

Captain Armand Pinsard

outer circle of closely-meshed barbed wire. The way to survive was to keep his spirits up. The war might be over before he could get out, and then it might not. In the days since he had been here, he had heard disturbing rumors of "prisoner's syndrome," men who could not cope, who threw themselves against the barbed wire in a hopeless fury of despair. He must not do that. He must keep cheerful. And keep a clear mind.

Pinsard did not wait long to try to rejoin the French Air Service. Between March, 1915, and the spring of 1916, he attempted multiple escapes: through a heating duct, in a garbage bin, via the sewers, in a laundry basket. Each time he was frustrated. For punishment, he and several other officers who attempted to escape found themselves confined in the medieval fortress at Ingolstadt. Security was heavy here. Shut up in a tower and allowed out only for roll-call, Pinsard had little hope of escape. If caught, he would be shot. But he refused to grow discouraged. A golf course is for golf. A tennis court is for tennis. A prison camp is for escaping.

It was that simple.

Absolutely without self-pity, he threw himself into his work. Taking another officer into his confidence, he plotted afresh. This time, they would tunnel beneath the twelve-foot-thick wall separating them from the world outside. They could only dig at night, after the guards had checked the room and called their names. Crawling on hands and knees, sometimes on his belly, Pinsard scraped out the earth with the aid of a soup tin and his bare hands. Finally, on March 26, 1916, they broke through to the rocky slope far enough beyond Ingolstadt to escape the sentries' gunfire. For two weeks, he worked his way through the dangerous countryside till at last he slipped over the border into Switzerland. After thirteen months of imprisonment, Pinsard was free. It was his first escape from prison, but it would not be his last.

In the months that followed, Pinsard received the rank of captain and flew solo for the foremost French fighter squadron. Once, he crashed with massive injuries. When he got out of the hospital, he painted his fighting plane black and renamed it "Revenge IV." Then in 1916, fact became fantasy. On an early November afternoon, the future film director Jean Renoir flew over Lechelle, snapping aerial photographs of the enemy position. Suddenly, a German Fokker swooped down on him. Before he could respond to the attack, a French pilot, invisible in the cockpit of a Spad VII roared in and shot the German down in flames, saving

Renoir's life. Twenty years later, the director and the pilot Armand Pinsard met again.

So impressed was Renoir with Pinsard's attitude towards his imprisonment that he based his great anti-war film, *Grand Illusion,* on the French pilot's story. Most people would have given up on life after more than a year in a German prison. But Armand Pinsard was unstoppable. By maintaining a good attitude in impossible circumstances, he was able to endure thirteen months in captivity and dig his way out to freedom—scoring a final Allied victory.

Then he said unto them, Go your way, eat the fat, and drink the sweet, and send portions unto them for whom nothing is prepared: for this day is holy unto our Lord: neither be ye sorry; for the joy of the Lord is your strength.

—Nehemiah 8:10

Questions

1. Explain how Lt. Pinsard came to be imprisoned.
2. What was his assigned job in the war?
3. Tell of his attempted escapes.
4. What was his attitude in prison? Did he intentionally work to maintain that?
5. How did his good attitude affect other prisoners?
6. Tell of his encounter with the filmmaker and what impressed him with Pinsard's attitude.
7. Why was he inspired to make a film about Pinsard?
8. How does your attitude affect those around you?
9. What can you do in your home and sphere of influence to promote joyfulness?
10. Think of an instance lately that provoked you to complain. What were the consequences of that attitude? What can you do the next time you face a similar circumstance?

Courage

DEFINITION

Standing alone for righteousness
and yielding my fears to God

MEMORY VERSE

Have not I commanded thee?
Be strong and of a good courage;
be not afraid, neither be thou dismayed;
for the Lord thy God is with thee
whithersoever thou goest.
Joshua 1:9

Casualty

Colonel Aleksandr Groten

World War I, The Russian Front

Autumn, 1915

The telephone call came through at 1500 hours. Rising from the muddy ground beside the machine-gun, Colonel Aleksandr Groten loosened his collar and gripped the receiver tightly. Shrapnel burst in the trees overhead, spraying his shoulder-boards with dirt.

"Groten speaking."

"What are you playing at?" Commander Menshikov's voice crackled over the wire. "I gave you orders to advance an hour ago."

An officer using a field telephone

Field telephones were rare and often defective. Last year, Second Army General Aleksandr Samsonov had only twenty-five telephones for his entire army. In the middle of the combat zone, buried lines snaked underground to avoid direct hits from heavy artillery shells. A second explosion burst somewhere in front of him. Groten jiggled the switch frantically and then handed it over to the army operator.

Disconnected.

In the rear, a huddle of dun-colored cavalry shifted and stamped under the hot sky. The field telephone shrilled again. Groten caught it on the next ring. "Sir, we are surrounded in a dense swamp and cannot advance without severe casualties."

He had to shout to make himself heard over the roar of the German 77 FK 96 field guns. Their own smaller 76.2 mm. guns popped in reply. "If I advance now, my entire unit will be wiped out. The *Nemetz* have posted their guns on higher ground—"

"I'm ordering you to advance at once, Colonel!" The commander's voice purpled. "Give me casualties, not topography."

Groten gritted his teeth. He would do his best. He forced himself to ease the telephone onto its hook and stood over it for several seconds, breathing heavily. Several men watched him with eyes like faded bluebells. How many children did they have?

He took his field glasses from the leather case at his side and trained on the still, black marsh between the scrubby pines. Then he stared up at the slope gouged by shell holes. The muzzles of the German guns, aiming over the hill, perched like black crows. Clouds of mosquitoes hung like pale gauze in the muggy air, stinging the soldiers' faces and hands. They would have to wade across 500 feet of open swamp, their rifles slung across their shoulders, the backs of their necks straight, clean-shaven, vulnerable. Groten closed his eyes. They could not creep around and flank the Germans from the rear. The swamp stretched before them for miles on either side.

When he opened his eyes, he said briefly: "Tell the *Hussars* to advance."

A metallic bugle note shimmered in the humid air. The *Hussars* in their crimson jackets with gold braid dismounted and began to pick their way across the marsh like ants. Mud sucked at their boots. Briars tore at their tight blue breeches.

The ground shook.

"Gospodi Pomeelui . . . Lord, have mercy on us."

Groten could feel the slow surge and murmur of humanity wading around him, about to be fed fodder into the war-machine by their commanders. They struggled out of sight into the dark mouth of the swamp. Death hovered over them, a double-headed eagle with black wings.

Drops of sweat broke out on his forehead.

Suddenly Groten shouted: "Call them back! I can't do it. If the General wants a casualty, I'll give him one."

If it's not too late.

Somewhere behind him, he heard the bugle frantically shrilling retreat. Shoulders erect, he stepped from behind his shelter and walked straight into enemy gunfire. Something slammed into him with a dull thud. He clapped a hand to his shoulder. Blood leaked hotly between his fingers. Swaying a little, he turned slowly towards his men.

"Very good. You can retire now."

He had a dim sense of bodies swirling past him, retrograding into the trees. Then his eyes hazed over. For a long time, there was nothing but the agonizing jolting of the cart, the dark tunnel of trees spiraling overhead, brilliant shafts of light. An aide rode beside him.

Groten spoke only once. "Are they safe?"

He meant his men.

"Yes, sir." The aide blinked back tears. "They pulled back an hour ago. You shouldn't have done it, Your Honor."

Groten closed his eyes. "I'm glad."

Headquarters was in an uproar. The General,

fretting constantly about his tired horses, lumbered down the steps to where Groten lay in the scanty shade of the field ambulance.

"You're crazy, Colonel. You could have been killed!"

Groten opened one cold grey eye. "I'm fine." His voice was dry. "But what do you mean, decimating my men?"

By exposing himself to certain death in order to save his soldiers, Colonel Aleksandr Groten demonstrated uncommon courage and self-sacrifice.

Then Peter and the other apostles answered and said, "We ought to obey God rather than men."

—Acts 5:29

Questions

1. How did Colonel Groten demonstrate supreme courage?
2. What did his commanding officer want him to do?
3. Why didn't he do it?
4. What did he suppose would happen if he had obeyed the order?
5. What do you suppose his men felt when he placed himself in the line of fire?
6. Why does it sometimes take more courage to obey God rather than men?
7. Think of an instance where you were afraid to do something. What might you do when faced with such a situation again?
8. Does having courage mean we are never afraid?
9. What would you do if your friends were all getting ready to do something wrong and wanted you to join them?

Loyalty

DEFINITION

Committed to the welfare
of those I serve,
even to the detriment
of my own comfort.

MEMORY VERSE

Most men will proclaim
their own goodness;
but a faithful man who can find?
Proverbs 20:6

Greater Love

Darya Efimova

The Russian Revolution, Petrograd
December, 1917

December 20, 1917. The Cheka (Russian secret police) came at night. Between the hours of ten and dawn, black limousines roamed the silent streets, headlights sweeping the windows and catching the faces of passersby like moths in the glare. At 2:00 a.m., the cook Darya Efimova sat straight up in bed. Her scarf slipped from her grey hair. What was going on? The little flat was bitterly cold. Outside, Kirochnaia Street was flooded with moonlight. The sound of knocking beat against her head. Someone was trying to break down the door.

Commissar Moisei Uritsky

Darya leaped out of bed. Peering through the doorway, she saw Colonel Andrei Kalpaschnikoff come out of his bedroom, thrusting his arms into the sleeves of his dressing gown. He looked tall, fair, and ghostly in the dim light. Quickly, he undid the bolts and slid back the chain. The door burst open and three semi-automatics bristled in his face. Beyond them, Darya could see 30 Red Guards in black leather jackets crowding the stairs, dirty sheepskin hats pushed back on their heads. Bayonet points flashed in the glow of a lamp swinging from a chain overhead. The Colonel stared at them, shivering slightly in his thin nightshirt.

Suddenly, a blond boy pressed his revolver against the Colonel's throat. The cold steel kissed his neck; his head jerked to one side. Darya's heart smothered. No, not the master! They couldn't kill him. The boy screamed. It was the scream of a panther.

"If you don't surrender, you are dead!"

Bewildered, the Colonel slowly raised his hands. He backed into the room, and the mob surged into the flat. And in that instant, Darya moved in a flash. *I've served the family for over fifty years. I lived with them at their country estate, cooking for them, nursing them, overseeing the servants. No one is going to hurt the master now.* She slipped into the bedroom, hastily cramming bits of gold jewelry, watches and silver spoons into hiding places.

Her ear was sharp. She listened to the snatches of conversation going on in the front room above the crash of furniture as sailors jerked out drawers, overturned tables and stuffed their pockets with knick-knacks, jewelry, leather gloves, and boots.

"Are you Colonel Andrei Kalpaschnikoff of the General Staff?" demanded the commissar.

The Colonel's voice was calm. "I am Kalpaschnikoff of the American Red Cross."

"You are the chief and soul of an American Plot."

"You're mistaken."

Someone bashed a hole in the wall with a rifle butt. Plaster dust rained down.

"In the name of the Council of the Commissioners, in the name of the Soviets which represent the Russian people, I declare you under arrest," the commissar barked. "I will give you several minutes in which to dress and you will be taken to the Fortress of St. Peter and St. Paul, where you will be immediately isolated in solitary confinement."

She caught her breath. The Fortress was a big, gloomy grey edifice, surrounded by water. The Neva River streams ran underground there; damp trickled continually down the cell walls, seeping into the prisoners' aching bones. Solitary confinement meant no light. No human voice to break the silence. Scarce food. Only rats and darkness and dripping water.

She heard the Colonel protest. "But—"

"Get dressed."

Commissar Blagonravov pulled out a chair and sat down at the desk. Throwing one leg over his knee, he opened his soft fur coat lined with sealskin, pulled sheaves of paper from the drawers and riffled through them. Darya burst into the dining room. Her cheeks blazed. She went right up to Blagonravov, who sat calmly smoking a cigarette, and shook her fist at him.

"You are a pack of robbers who are only here under the pretext of requisition to steal anything you can lay your hands on!"

Blagonravov leaped up. He seized her by the shoulders, gripping so hard that it hurt. His teeth shone wolfishly.

"Now look here, woman, if you don't shut up, I shall have you also arrested."

She jerked her chin back. "You can cut my head off if you want to," she shouted. "But I, Darya, faithful servant of the Kalpaschnikoff family, tell you that the Bolsheviks are murderers and thieves who disgrace the Russian people!"

Sudden tears ran down her cheeks. She turned towards the Colonel, holding out her hands. "Imagine what they have done! They have taken the beautiful American shoes you brought me from New York.

Isn't that awful? I shall never get another pair like that."

It hurt to lose those shoes, real American shoes that cost $6.50. Not only because she had never had anything like them in her life before, but because the Colonel had given them to her. She had been so busy concealing his things that she forgot about her own.

Blagonravov glanced away from her. Then he strode to the door and bellowed to the sailors to clear out.

He returned, shrugging. "I can't help it if my men take a few things while they are doing their work. Everything has to be carefully verified in this flat. I know that a lot of weapons and documents are hidden here."

The Colonel, with his coat thrown around his shoulders, was pushed to the door. Darya tugged at the commissar's arm.

"Can't he take any food or warm clothes with him?"

"Not now," Blagonravov said. "We will see later, although I think he will never want anything again."

He laughed, and the sound chilled Darya.

They were going to kill him.

Behind her, the search went on. Workmen unscrewed the curtains, stripped out the lining and inspected the seams. They ripped open the covers of chairs and couches, knocked out the glass from mirrors and photograph frames, tore up the floorboards. But Darya was old and frail now. What was she going to do without him? How would he survive without food or blankets?

She clutched his hands, but he went away from her, down the dark, dirty staircase lined by Red Guards. In the hall below, two men lay with the muzzles of automatic guns aimed at the Colonel's chest. He would not try to run.

Darya ran to the window just as a sleek black limousine purred up to the curb. The door opened, exposing seats covered with yellow silk. She watched as they shoved her master inside, followed by Blagonravov and two guards. Four Latvians, armed with bayonets, jumped onto the running-boards as the car lurched off into the night. They passed the British Embassy on the embankment and swung towards Trinity Bridge.

The soldiers searched the flat for incriminating documents until 6 p.m. on December 21. Sixteen hours. Then they were gone. For weeks, Darya guarded the flat like a bloodhound. She spent hours on her knees, scrubbing the floor and worrying. What will they do to him? She must help him. But how? She filled a tub with warm water, lifted the Colonel's white Spitz puppy into it and began to soap him down. Suddenly, the telephone rang. Darya struggled up from her knees, wiping her hands on her dress. She lifted the receiver.

"Is that Darya Efimova?"

She did not recognize the voice.

"Yes, I am Darya." She spoke carefully.

"This is the headquarters of the Soviet Police. We want to talk to you."

That was enough. She began to shout.

"You are nothing but a gang of robbers and murderers! You arrested my master and you should give back the things you stole."

"You had better be careful what you say," buzzed an angry voice. "I am Uritsky, the Commissar of Justice, and if you insult me, I shall have you arrested."

Darya was too indignant to think. "I am not afraid of you! I am a poor woman, but for me you are murderers and burglars who have stolen my yellow shoes, my beautiful yellow shoes."

This was the way to make them listen. To accuse them about the shoes.

"What shoes?" Moisei Uritsky demanded in astonishment.

Her voice shrilled: "You all have no consciences, just because some fool invented some stupid stories about my good master; here in front of me, your Red Guards arrested him, raided the flat, and stuck in their pockets the present he brought me from America."

"What!" Uritsky shouted.

"Yes, the beautiful yellow shoes." She sobbed.

There was silence on the other end of the line. Then the Bolshevik laughed. His tone softened. "Darya, don't be so angry and don't weep over your things."

"It isn't funny," she retorted.

"It's all right," he consoled her. "We'll find your shoes for you." However, he had called about an entirely different matter. The Cheka recently arrested a young officer on the next floor who stole money to fund the anti-Bolshevik "Direct Anarchist" society. Since Darya often cleaned his room and given him tea, they wanted to ask her some questions about him.

Go to the Cheka station? It was miles away.

"No," she said promptly. "I'm going to wash my master's dog. I cannot run so far on foot."

Uritsky said quickly, "I wouldn't dream of keeping you long! So as not to waste time, I'll send my private car for you. It will pick you up and bring you back."

A few minutes later, a black Packard roared up and parked in front of No. 11 Kirochnaia Street. Wearing a black silk handkerchief over her head and carrying the Colonel's dog in her arms, Darya sailed down the stairs. The chauffer snapped to attention. Darya settled her skirts in the vehicle. The doors shut. People ran out of the house to look. The hall porter gaped. She was no longer a simple peasant woman. She was an important witness. As she glanced up at the windows, she could almost see her master's tall, thin figure floating like a ghost behind the glass.

Soon a grey building loomed up on Gurokhovaia Street: the dungeons of the secret police. Darya stood calmly in the waiting room, listening for her name. She did not have to wait long.

The door to Uritsky's office opened.

"Darya Efimova!"

Taking her courage in both hands, she crossed the dirty floor covered with spittle. Her shoes crunched on the shells of sunflower seeds. The door closed behind her. She was in Uritsky's den. Darya bowed deeply from the waist, her eyes searching the corner opposite the door for the holy icon. Her eyes met instead the oblique, black gaze of Vladimir Lenin. Then she looked up and saw Uritsky's flat, clean-shaven face and curving nose.

"Good morning, *Barin* (Master)." Her voice was soft, rural, the vowels drawn out in the village fashion.

Uritsky looked startled over his pince-nez (eye glasses). Masters and tsars, laws and police no longer existed. But he looked pleased. This was a very dignified old woman.

Her eyes searched his face. "You look like a good *barin.* You do not look wicked at all, and now that I have seen you, I really do not understand why people are not ashamed to [insult you], ready to strangle everyone."

Her voice was soft and coaxing, her gaze direct. It was as if Uritsky was seeing himself for the first time. What if he did sign hundreds of death sentences every day? He was the Commissar of Justice. He had power over life and death.

He brought her a chair.

Please to sit down.

"Now that you are in a good temper," he began ingratiatingly, "I want you to be a good woman and tell me everything about the officer who lived in your house." He paused. "If you read these papers we found and tell me everything, I will help recover the stolen things and I myself will search for the yellow shoes."

Darya protested that she could not read. But she would tell what she had seen. As she finished her story, they brought the guilty officer into the room. Slowly, Darya stood up. Here was a man arrested for doing the same thing the Red Guards had done: stealing.

"It might be pardoned in a simple peasant or Bolshevik—" her voice rose scornfully—"but for an officer, it was a shame to do such things. My master would never have tried to steal! He would have preferred to die of hunger or have his hands cut off rather than touch what did not belong to him."

They were listening, now.

Her voice thickened. "My master, who has never done any harm except helping the poor people, is in prison on unjust accusations and rascals like you are running loose, committing all kinds of crime."

She didn't care what happened to her. She had turned the tables on them, made them see the truth.

"You, who are a good *barin,* ought to see the

difference between such scamps and nice people like my master."

They couldn't stop her. The words poured on. Good must conquer evil. People must listen to the truth. She believed this.

An hour later, she sat in the apartment with two of Uritsky's chauffeurs wearing black leather jackets. She poured hot water from the samovar's spout, set out plates of biscuits and spooned dollops of sugary jam into their tea. All the while, she spoke gently, persuasively about her master. What a good man he was, how he worked for the Red Cross, helping wounded soldiers and distributing food to the starving peasants. They listened, their faces growing warm from the tea and from the words. It was getting dark, now. Darya leaned over to light the oil lamp before the big picture of St. Nicholas. The two men bowed deeply. At the door, they turned to look back at her. They felt sorry for the Colonel, now. He oughtn't to be in prison at all.

The next day, one of them came back. He had spoken to Uritsky and reminded him of his promise to help Darya Efimova. He came back often in the following weeks and months. Sometimes he secretly gave Darya information about the Communists.

Then suddenly, Colonel Kalpaschnikoff was released. Brought into the office of the Cheka, he stood before Uritsky. Pale and gaunt from months in prison, he could not understand the reason for this visit. Uritsky spoke to him one minute, shouted into the telephone the next.

"I told you to shoot them and not to annoy me any more about these men!"

The Colonel stood silently.

Dismissing the executions with a wave of his hand, Uritsky spun towards him.

"I shall certainly try to do something for you. I promised to do so for Comrade Efimova."

"My cook!" The Colonel was astonished.

"Yes, Darya." Uritsky smiled. "She is your best lawyer."

Colonel Kalpaschnikoff was released ten days later.

For weeks, he found it difficult to sleep in a soft bed. He was always expecting a cell door to clang, to wake up and find he was back in the Fortress. Then on August 17, 1918, a young military cadet assassinated Uritsky for the execution of his officer friends. Darya knew that her master would never be safe while he stayed in the country. The next day, the chauffer arrived with the news that Kalpaschnikoff's name was on a secret list of eighty-four people to be shot in the morning for Uritsky's murder. The plan to go to America began. Darya sent a little girl from the next flat out to buy an international train ticket. She poured the master a last cup of coffee. Then they sat down in the silent dining room to wait. An hour later the girl scrambled up the stairs, clutching the ticket. The Colonel's passport now listed him as a Communist battalion leader—not an enemy of the state.

The candle flame sputtered as Darya locked the door. "God will protect you," she whispered. "I shall continue to pray."

They went softly downstairs. Darya carried a big basket stuffed with food and clothing for the journey. She would not let him go like that again. As she distracted the ticket-seller at the bustling station, Colonel Kalpaschnikoff slipped onto the train. If he could cross the border to the Ukraine in the south, he would be safe.

Late that night, black motor cars from the Cheka roared down Kirochnaia Street and men in peaked caps surrounded No. 11. They found the flat empty, the bird flown. Darya, doddering out of bed in her shawl, obligingly showed them the house. She opened the cellar. She guided them around. Suddenly, the commissar noticed that she was smiling. Her face shone softly, contentedly through its network of wrinkles.

"Where is he? If you don't tell us, we will force you to speak."

She looked at him calmly. "What can you do to me, if I persist in hiding my master?"

"Arrest you as a counter-revolutionist!" snarled the commissar.

Darya smiled quietly. "I am not afraid of you. I am a simple peasant; you have no right to do anything to me. I shall nevertheless give you the necessary information. Mr. Kalpaschnikoff is in Finland, on his way to America." That was directly north; he had gone south. "He has gone to fetch me another pair of yellow shoes to replace the ones you stole the first time you grabbed him. It is too late, you cannot catch him anymore."

It was the last thing she could do for him. The man she had nursed, carried in her arms, sweated and cared for, was safe.

She could smile at anything.

They seized her arms and dragged her down to the car. At two o'clock that morning, the Bolsheviks shot eighty-three of the eighty-four people on their list. Only Colonel Kalpaschnikoff escaped. Darya Efimova spent a month in the same Fortress as her beloved master. In four weeks, she was transferred to an unknown place to be released. After that, she disappeared from history into the heavy snows, the meadows of birch trees, the language and color of the people she loved so devotedly.

History is not only made by people like George Washington or Abraham Lincoln. Common people, their commitment and faith comprise the backbone of history. Darya Efimova showed uncommon loyalty to those the family she served, even if it cost her her life.

Questions

1. Tell of Darya's loyalty to her master.
2. What was Colonel Kalpaschnikoff accused of? By whom?
3. Tell of Kalpaschnikoff's capture. How did Darya try to prevent it?
4. What role did Darya play in his release from prison?
5. How did her master escape?
6. What had his job been?
7. What was Darya's fate?
8. Why was she still happy amidst such adverse circumstances?
9. What family/friends do you need to show loyalty to?
10. What are some specific ways you could demonstrate loyalty this week?

Obedience

DEFINITION

Doing what is expected of me cheerfully, immediately, and thoroughly

MEMORY VERSE

Children, obey your parents in all things: for this is well pleasing unto the Lord.

Colossians 3:20

Argonne Forest

Sergeant Alvin C. York

World War I, Argonne Forest, France

October 18, 1918

Chatel Chehery: October 8, 1918. This felt like Armageddon. The last battle between angels and demons. The stark, shredded trees burned below him with a blinding glow, stretching fearful fingers to the night sky. The flash and belch of artillery cut through the rainy mist to the steep, wooded valley beyond the hill of Montfaucon. Shells exploded around him in the dawn, tearing up the ground. Horses thrashed and whinnied in the road. The sound carried through the cold, damp air like glass ringing. Men sprawled in heaps like dead leaves, Bavarians in dark blue coats, Saxons in sky-blue tunics, Austrians in silver, British and Americans in yellow khaki and the French in smoky-blue.

Sgt. Alvin C. York

It had rained all day, a drizzling, penetrating rain that soaked Corporal Alvin C. York's greatcoat, dripped from his reddish mustache and turned his tattered puttees into strips of wet cardboard. Often during these dark days, American soldiers could be heard chanting:

"We're all going calling on the Kaiser,
For we've got to teach the Kaiser to be wiser."

But the forest was worse. The cabin in the mountains of Pall Mall, Tennessee, and Gracie Williams blurred in Sgt. York's mind. The locals knew him at age twenty-seven as a hard-drinker and hard-fighter, as well as a deadly accurate shot at local turkey shoots. Then he met God and Gracie Williams and everything changed. He gave his life over to Christ. But when America entered World War I on the Allied side, he found that he did not believe in the war. "I was worried clean through," he said. "I didn't want to go and kill. I believed in my Bible."

Then on June 5, 1917, he registered for the draft. On his draft card they had printed the question: "Do you claim exemption from draft?" He wrote: "Yes. Don't want to fight."

The army denied his claim. When York received the news, he filed an appeal. Few things in the military atmosphere of 1917 were more unpopular than a conscientious objector. The other recruits viewed such men as cowards and treated them harshly. The army looked down on them, but forced them to work in non-combatant roles. While York's petition was still under review, he entered the service at Camp Gordon, Georgia. During those weeks of boot-camp, York spoke with his commanding officer, Major Buxton, who urged him seek the Bible and pray about his doubts. Finally, alone on a mountaintop, York came to the conclusion that it was his moral duty to participate in the war. From the time he went to France, he never looked back.

Russia, with the connivance of the Bolshevik Party at the Treaty of Brest-Litovsk, had dropped out of the war in March. The Germans now occupied most of Eastern Europe as well as France and Belgium. On the western front, the lines had only advanced a mile or two since 1914.

The Meuse–Argonne offensive began on the 26th of September, 1918. According to Marshal Ferdinand Foch's strangling offensive, Belgian, British, and French forces drove through Flanders to the north, pushing the Germans ahead of them. At the same time, British troops hit the center, attacking all along the Hindenburg Line: a four-mile deep barricade of steel and concrete fortifications. Meanwhile, to the south, the French Fourth Army with General Henri Gourand and the American First Army under General John "Black Jack" Pershing would face the most difficult stretch of all. Striking between the old cathedral town of Reims and the shattered walls of Verdun, the soldiers fought along the bank of the Meuse and plunged into the Argonne Forest. In the heart of the forest, the German lines lay 12 miles deep. Trenches, bunkers, and defense wire rusting there for four years blocked their way. But the combined attack succeeded.

The night before, York slept with his men in the Zona Woods. Only a few splintered trees gaped over their heads. He knew that they had not reached the real fighting yet. Since October 4th, the Americans continued to throw themselves in dangerous frontal assaults at the impregnable Hindenburg Line perched on the ridge at Romagne. During the afternoon of October 7th, York and the other members of the American Expeditionary Force lay on their bellies in shallow holes in the roadside for hours. German airplanes with silver crosses on the wings swooped overhead with a buzz like angry hornets. Night fell as he stared at the burning woods. Somewhere in there was the Lost Battalion. This group of 650 soldiers of the 75th Division had disappeared into the heavily-guarded No-Man's land between Bois d'Apremont and Charlevaux earlier in the fighting on October 2nd. No one had come back.

Before dawn on October 8th, York, Sergeant Bernard Early, and sixteen men set off for the Decauville railroad. Their mission: to take out the machine guns on Hill 223 in the Chatel-Chehery sector of the Meuse-Argonne sector. The four non-commissioned officers crouched over their map, trying to decipher the unfamiliar French names. Then they set off again, crawling through the wooded terrain full of shattered stumps. Guns thundered overhead.

Suddenly, yellow gas began to creep toward them. It came at them like an olive-green cloud, rolling over the ground. Yellowish-green, it grew darker where it spread along the ground, thinning out to a thin grey near the top. It made your eyes burn, gripped your stomach, tore at your lungs. Mustard gas was the most easily recognized. Chlorine gas, colorless and deadly, could kill a man before he knew it. At Ypres in 1916, they had had nothing to cover their mouths with except pieces of cloth smeared with mud. Now, grabbing his gas mask and fastening the goggles and straps, York dashed for Hill 223.

American soldiers carrying M1917 rifles with bayonets

Crossing the flat, snow-covered expanse, barren of any life except for the unseen snipers, they stumbled through weedy brush towards the low hill. Soldiers fell like cut grass before the pounding machine guns. They would have to sneak around and take the gun nests from the rear.

It was after 6:00 a.m. They continued crawling deep into the brush. Three hundred yards beyond their front lines, they stopped near the top of the hill and conferred. Some wanted to attack the Germans from the flank. But York knew that they had to spring on them from the rear. Inching forward again, they found themselves behind enemy lines. They could not see the Germans and the Germans could not see them. Sharp firing broke out in the woods as York and his men leaped across a thin stream. On the other side, twenty Germans threw up their hands.

"Kamerad!" they shouted. "Comrade!"

They had landed in the middle of the Landwehr Infantry headquarters. German helmets poked up from the bunkers like sitting ducks. They had breakfast spread out, a jumble of jams, jellies, beefsteaks, and loaves of bread. They were just tucking in when York burst into camp.

"Put 'em up!" he ordered.

They stuck their hands over their heads without muttering. Within minutes, the large German force, thinking the entire American army was behind them, surrendered. Suddenly, the German major shouted something in guttural tones. All at once, the German machine guns on the hill swung their snouts towards them. A murderous spat of gunfire burst out of the woods less than thirty yards away. All but two of York's squad toppled instantly. Sergeant Early went down with three bullets, leaving York in command. Brush whizzed past him. He had no time to dodge behind a tree. Instead, he began shooting back at the thirty gunners firing continuously at him.

"I had no time nohow to do nothing but watch them-there German machine gunners and give them the best I had," he said. "Every time I seed a German I jes' teched him off. At first I was shooting from a prone position; that is lying down; jes' like we often shoot at the targets in the shooting matches in the mountains of Tennessee . . . But the targets here were bigger. I jes' couldn't miss a German's head or body at that distance. And I didn't. Besides, it weren't no time to miss nohow. I knowed that in order to shoot me, the Germans would have to get their heads up to see where I was lying. And I knowed that my only chance was to keep their heads down. And I done done it. I covered their positions and let fly every time I seed anything to shoot at. Every time a head come up I done knocked it down. Then they would sorter stop for a moment and then another head would come up and I would knock it down, too. I was giving them the best I had."

All the time, York kept yelling at them to come down. He did not want to kill any more men than he had to. His rifle barrel scorched his hands. He had only half a cartridge clip left in his M1917 Enfield rifle, but he flipped out his .45 Colt automatic pistol just as German Lieutenant Paul Jümer Vollmer and five soldiers vaulted out of a ditch twenty-five yards away. They charged at him with fixed bayonets. Aiming calmly, York picked off the last one first, all the way up the line. It was just like shooting turkeys back home: if you shot the last one first, the other ones didn't know and kept on going. Vollmer shot at him again and again, but he could not hit York. Then the German major scrambled up from the ground and came towards him.

"English?" he shouted.

York shook his head. "No, not English."

"What?" he demanded.

"American."

The major sighed with relief. "Good! If you won't shoot any more, I will make them give up."

Twenty German soldiers lay sprawled on the ground. York did not trust the major. He kept his automatic trained on him while the major gave a sharp little whistle. Instantly, the Germans threw down their guns and belts. But as they started back over the hill, one of them lobbed a hand-grenade at York. It burst in the air, scattering bits of shrapnel. York had to "tech him off."

Everyone held up their hands then. With only seven men left, he lined the Germans up in two rows and made them carry the American wounded out. Placing the German major at the front of the column, York kept his pistol pressed tight to his back. Suddenly, the major suggested going down a nearby gully. With a tingle in his veins, York knew that this was a trap. Instead, he nudged the German officer ahead of him. They were going back to the American front straight through the German lines. On the way, he kept collecting Germans like butterflies. Close to Chatel Chehery, the party came under heavy shell fire. York had to double-quick the prisoners through the area to make sure that he did not lose any of them. They had surrendered, and it was up to him to keep them safe.

Sgt. York being congratulated after the war.

Back at headquarters, Brigadier General Lindsey greeted him: "Well, York, I hear you captured the whole German army."

York told him he had only 132.

The entire time, he had felt a deep, sweet calm. He gave the glory to God: "So you can see here in this case of mine where God helped me out. I had been living for God and working in the church some time before I come to the army. So I am a witness to the fact that God did help me out of that hard battle; for the bushes were shot up all around me and I never got a scratch. So you can see that God will be with you if you will only trust Him; and I say that He did save me."

The next morning, the 328th Regiment went in and found twenty-eight German soldiers lying behind the second line. Sergeant York's actions helped silence thirty-five machine guns and clear the way for fresh American troops to follow. Though he was only one man in one place, his actions gave a tremendous boost to morale. For his heroism, York won the Medal of Honor, the Distinguished Service Medal and the French Croix de Guerre and Legion of Honor.

Alvin C. York demonstrated obedience by carrying out orders in spite of his own feelings.

The fear of God makes a hero; the fear of man makes a coward.

—Sgt. Alvin York

Questions

1. Why did Alvin register as a conscienctious objector?
2. What happened to change his mind about that?
3. What was the mission of Sgt. Early's men?
4. How did they manage to capture the first 20 men?
5. What happened to leave command to Alvin York?
6. How did York's experience shooting turkeys back home aid him in this campaign?
7. How many prisoners did York end up capturing?
8. Tell how he gave the glory to God.
9. How many machine guns did York end up silencing?
10. What medals did Alvin York receive?
11. Explain how York demonstrated obedience to his orders despite his own feelings.
12. Describe how his obedience affected so many others.
13. Think of how you can do a better job at demonstrating obedience in your life.

Compassion

DEFINITION

Being willing to expend effort to help alleviate the suffering of those in need

MEMORY VERSE

Withhold not good from them to
whom it is due, when it is in the power
of thine hand to do it.
Say not to thy neighbor, Go, and
come again, and tomorrow I will give;
when thou hast it by thee.

Proverbs 3:27-28

Felt Boots

Gregory Burmistr

Nizhniy Novgorod, Russia
March 1919

In October, the skies closed over like a grey slate, people began shutting up their houses and the roads turned to ice. Zhenya didn't need boots, then. In November, the first snow fell, and still Zhenya had no boots. Father was away on one of those trips that grew more frequent since the civil war began. She often felt like an orphan since Father married their servant girl, Mania.

They were moving house today, because it cost too much to rent the house they lived in—the place

Zhenya thought of as home. At dawn, Zhenya and Mania tramped across the fields to look at the cottage. There were bedsteads to load, benches, clothes and blankets to pack. Gregory Burmistr, a local peasant, had offered to come along and help.

Strips of snow still lay in the fields. Zhenya, stepping carefully to avoid the deep puddles, scanned the countryside. Cattle with skeleton-thin ribs pawed hungrily at the yellow grass beneath the thin crust of snow. The wind tore at her sheepskin coat and her leaky boots sopped up the slushy snow, making her feel like she was barefoot. Mania, wearing heavy waterproof boots, did not seem to notice. It was too early for the buttercups to be out, though there was a sharp smell in the air as if the earth was waking up. But no sign of it yet. Not till mid-May.

Zhenya shivered. The others were far ahead of her now; black dots on a grey landscape. It was as if she were alone in the great, wide world, with nothing but the wind blowing and a bird sailing high like a scrap of paper against the clouds.

"Have you no other shoes, Bebby?"

Gregory Burmistr had turned back. Now he crouched in front of her, a big burly man in a tattered sheepskin coat. His eyes were gentle, sea-grey. She knew Burmistr slightly—a hard-working, God-fearing peasant who had built up a farmstead and mercantile business with his bare hands. But he was poor now. The same revolution that swept in like a whirlwind, promising peace and prosperity, had confiscated his house and land, and left him staring into a bleak spring.

"Don't you have any other shoes?"

"Why, no, Gregory." Zhenya felt cold water trickling against her toes. "It will be summer soon; these will last till then."

But summer was months away. If Father came home, there would be fields of yellow daisies, children playing, and barefoot days. Summer was a magical time. Everything would be all right when summer came.

But Gregory was looking at her.

"Hmm." He shut his eyes as if thinking. The wind tossed his black beard. Without another word, he caught up to Mania, telling some joke which Zhenya did not catch, its end blown away by the wind.

The next day, Gregory brought her a pair of felt boots with elastic sides. Zhenya gasped. Though second-hand, they shone with careful polishing, and their soles were clean and whole. Only Gregory had known how she dreaded living in the village without a decent pair of shoes.

In April, Father came home. After the long winter, Zhenya no longer needed the boots. It was barefoot time. The rains came and the revolution passed over their heads and was gone, leaving a thundering silence in its wake.

But Zhenya never forgot Gregory Burmistr.

Gregory Burmistr demonstrated generosity by giving his last pair of boots to a child when he himself was in need.

Give of yourself, give as much as you can! And you can always, always give something, even if it is only kindness! If everyone were to do this and would not be as mean with a kindly word, then there would be much more justice and love in the world. Give and you shall receive, much more than you would have ever thought possible. Give, give again and again, don't lose courage, keep it up and go on giving! No one has ever become poor from giving!

—Anne Frank, the essay "Give" from The Works of Anne Frank

Questions

1. Explain Zhenya's many hardships.
2. What was her need that Gregory Burmistr discovered?
3. What had caused the people to become poor?
4. Where was Zhenya's father?
5. How did Gregory Burmistr demonstrate compassion to the girl?
6. How did it affect Zhenya?
7. Sometimes acts of compassion are little things, but become milestones in the live of the receiver. Think of someone to whom you could show compassion. Work out a plan to implement it.
8. How can a simple act of compassion become a motivator in someone else's life?

Selected Bibliography

Andreyev, Ivan. *Russia's Catacomb Saints: Lives of the New Martyrs*. California: Saint Herman of Alaska Press, 1982.

Bashkiroff, Zenaide. *Nights Are Longest There: A Young Girl's Account of Revolution in Russia*. London: M. Spearman, 1960.

Berkin, Carol. *Revolutionary Mothers: Women in the Struggle for America's Independence*. Vintage Press, 2006.

Bruce, Philip Alexander. *Brave Deeds of Confederate Soldiers*. Harrisonburg: Sprinkle Publications, 2006.

Caldwell, Charles. *Memoirs of the Life and Campaigns of the Honorable Nathaniel Greene, Major General in the Army of the United States and Commander of the Southern Department in the War of the Revolution*. Philadelphia: Robert Desilver, printer, 1810. Reprint. Nabu Press, 2010.

Callo, Joseph. *John Paul Jones: America's First Sea Warrior.* Naval Institute Press, 2006.

Cheripko, Jan. *Caesar Rodney's Ride Eighty Miles for Freedom*. Boyd's Mill Press, 2004 (Grades 3-6).

Davis, Burke. *To Appomattox: Nine April Days, 1865*. New York: Rinehart & Company, 1959.

Delaplaine, Edward S. *Francis Scott Key: Life and Times*. Heritage Books, 2011.

Driggs, Laurence La Tourette. *Heroes of Aviation*. Little, Brown and Company, 1918 (Armand Pinsard).

Elliot, Elisabeth. *A Chance to Die: The Life and Legacy of Amy Carmichael*. Revell Press, 2005.

Fluckey, Eugene. *Thunder Below! The USS "Barb" Revolutionizes Submarine Warfare in World War II*. University of Illinois Press, 1997. "The Flying Panther: Captain Edward J. Simpson." *American Aviation Society*, 2011.

Fougara, Katherine Gibson. *With Custer's Cavalry*. Iyer Press, 2007.

Franklin, Benjamin. *Benjamin Franklin's Autobiography*. W.W. Norton & Company, 1986.

Franks, Norman, and Harry Dempsey. *Nieuport Aces of World War I. Osprey Aircraft of the Aces*, No. 33. Osprey Publishing, 2000 (Armand Pinsard).

Gaustad, Edwin S. *Liberty of Conscience: Roger Williams in America*. Judson Press, 1999.

______________ *Roger Williams*. New York: Oxford University Press, 2005.

Gilmer, George R. *Sketches of Some of the First Settlers of Upper Georgia, of the Cherokees, and the Author.* New York 1855, 1926, p. 90 (Reprinted in 1965 by Genealogical Publishing Co., Baltimore, and 1989 by Heritage Papers, Danielsville, Georgia).

Goodyear, Robert C. *The Real Pennsylvania Dutch American, "Molly Pitcher": A Documented History.* Author House, 2012 (Suggested reading).

Grack-Koestler, Rachel A. *Molly Pitcher: Heroine of the War for Independence*. Chelsea House Publications, 2005.

Green, Roger. *The Life and Ministry of William Booth: Founder of the Salvation Army*. Abingdon Press, 2006.

Hattersley, Roy. *Blood and Fire: The Story of William and Catherine Booth and the Salvation Army*. New York: Doubleday, 2000.

Hearn, Chester G. *Tracks in the Sea: Matthew Fontaine Maury and the Mapping of the Oceans*. International Marine Press, 2003.

Hembree, Charles R. *From Pearl Harbor to the Pulpit: The Dramatic Story of Captain Fuchida and Jacob DeShazer*. Akron, Ohio: Rex Humbard World Wide Ministry, 1975.

Hocker, Edward W. *The Fighting Parson of the American Revolution: A Biography of General Peter Muhlenberg, Lutheran Clergyman, Military Chieftain and Political Leader*. Philadelphia: Edward W. Hocker, 1936.

Holt, Rackham Vincent. *George Washington Carver: An American Biography*. New York: Doubleday, 1963.

Hull, Michael D. *Peter Francisco: American Revolutionary War Hero. Military History Magazine*, July-August, 2006.

Kackley, Paul. "The Dead Yank Hero of Orleans Forest." *Stars and Stripes*, 25 Nov. 1959.

Kalpaschnikoff, Andrei. *A Prisoner of Trotsky's*. New York: Doubleday Page, 1920.

Kidd, Thomas S. *Patrick Henry: First Among Patriots*. Basic Books, 2011.

Knight, Lucien. *Georgia's Landmarks, Memorials, and Legends*. Penguin Publishing, 2006 (Nancy Morgan Hart).

Lewis, Meriwether. *Original Journals of the Lewis and Clark Expedition, 1804-1806*. New York: Arno Press, 1969.

Littauer, V. S. *Russian Hussar*. London: J. A. Allen, 1965.

Marks, Lara. "Sacagawea as an Evolving Symbol of American Indian Women." Dec. 16, 1998.

Marshall, Charles. *An Aide-de-Camp of Lee*. Kessinger Publishing, 2007.

Muhlenberg, Henry A. *The Life of Major-General Peter Muhlenberg, of the Revolutionary Army*. Philadelphia: Carey and Hart, 1849.

Perry, John. *Sergeant York: His Life, Legend and Legacy: The Remarkable Untold Story of Sergeant Alvin C. York*. Barnes and Noble Books, 1997.

Phelps, M. William. *Nathan Hale: The Life and Death of America's First Spy*. Thomas Dunne Books, 2008.

Polsky, Michael. *The New Martyrs of Russia*. Montreal: The Saint Job of Pochaev Brotherhood, 2002.

Ramage, James A. *Grey Ghost: The Life of Colonel John Singleton Mosby*. University of Kentucky Press, 2009.

Rappleye, Charles. *Robert Morris: Financier of the American Revolution*. New York: Simon & Schuster, 2010.

Salisbury, Gay and Laney Salisbury. *The Cruelest Miles: The Heroic Story of Dogs and Men in a Race Against an Epidemic*. New York: W. W. Norton & Company, 2005.

San Souci, Robert D. *Kate Shelley: Bound for Legend*. Dial Books for Young Readers, 1995. Scott, Jane. *A Gentleman as Well as a Whig, Caesar Rodney and the American Revolution*. University of Delaware Press, 2000.

Scott, John Thomas. "Nancy Hart: 'Too Good Not to Tell Again.' "*Georgia Women: Their Lives and Times*, vol.1. Chirhart, Ann Short, and Betty Wood, Ed. Athens: University of Georgia Press, 2009.

Silcox-Jarrett, Diane. *Heroines of the American Revolution: America's Founding Mothers*. Scholastic, Inc., 2000 (Lydia Darraugh).

Skeyhill, Tom. *Sergeant York and the Great War*. The Vision Forum, Inc., 1998.

Snow, William P. *Lee and His Generals*. New York: The Fairfax Press, 1982.

Strachey, Lytton. *Queen Victoria: An Eminent Illustrated Biography*. New York: Black Dog & Leventhal Publishers, 1998.

Summers, Julie. *The Colonel of Tamarkan: Philip Toosey and the Bridge on the River Kwai*. London: Simon & Schuster, 2005.

Thomas, Evan. *John Paul Jones: Sailor, Hero, Father of the American Navy*. New York: Simon & Schuster, 2003.

Vaughan, David J. *Give Me Liberty: The Christian Patriotism of Patrick Henry* (Leaders in Action). Cumberland House Publishing, 2002.

Walker, Gary C. *Civil War Tales: Volume II*. A & W Enterprise, 1994.

Washington, Booker T. *Up from Slavery*. New York: Dover Publications, 1995.

Waters-Power, Alma. *Virginia Giant: The Story of Peter Francisco*. New York: E.P. Dutton, 1957.

Wellman, Sam. *George Washington Carver: Inventor and Naturalist*. Barbour Publishing, 1998.

Wetterer, Margaret K. *Kate Shelley and the Midnight Express*. Scholastic, 1990.

Williams, Roger. *A Plea for Religious Liberty* in: *The Bloudy Tenant of Persecution*. Providence, Rhode Island: Narragansett Club, Vol. III, 1867.

Wrangel, Peter N. *Always with Honor*. New York: Robert Speller and Sons, 1957.

Websites

"Bill Overstreet." http://www.cebudanderson.com/billoverstreet.htm

"Bill Overstreet, 363rd FS." http://www.cebudanderson.com/overstreet.Htm

"Bill Overstreet: Barnstormers." http://www.barnstormers.com/eFLYER/2009/061-eFLYER-FA02-Legends-Overstreet.html

Winstead, Jane. "Horatio G. Spafford: The Story Behind the Hymn 'It is Well with My Soul.' " http://voices.yahoo.com/horatio-g-spafford-story-behind-hymn-is-1620793.html?cat=38.

Image Credits

Compassion

Aleksandr Ustinovich, 1994 • "A Road": http://01varvara.wordpress.com/2010/06/14/aleksandr-ustinovicha-road-1994/aleksandr-ustinovich-a-road-1994/

Contentment

Horatio and Anna Spafford: Public Domain. Wikimedia Commons: This work has been released into the public domain by its author, Live or die.

Shipwreck: Library of Congress: Library of Congress, Prints and Photographs Division: LC-DIG-ppmsca-07650, Currier & Ives

American Colony: Wikipedia.com: Public Domain because it is taken from the American Colony Archive

Courage

Colonel Aleksandr Groten

Officer with phone: An officer in a trench on the Eastern Front communicates via a field telephone, Bisecky Collection, Prague, 2009, Source, www.praguepost.com.jpg

Army in trenches: Public Domain. The Russian army in the trenches near Sarikamish. United Kingdom Government photograph. Public domain.jpg

Hospitality

Fort Abraham Lincoln: National Park Service, http://www.nps.gov/history/history/online_books/soldier/sitec12.htm (Minnesota Historical Society).

Native American child: Public Domain. Library of Congress, LC-USZC4-8846.

Joyfulness

Armand Pinsard: Public Domain. http://www.firstworldwar.com/bio/pinsard.htm

Loyalty

Commissar Moisei Uritsky: Public Domain. http://www.nasledie-rus.ru/img/660000/661307.jpg

Meekness

George Washington Carver: Public Domain. Library of Congress

Carver laboratory: Public Domain. US Department of Agriculture

Equipment: Public Domain. wikimedia.org/wikipedia/en/f/ff/George_Washington_Carver-laboratory_equipment.jpeg

Obedience

Sgt. Alvin C. York: Argonne Forest:The_National_Archives,_Series,_Signal_Corps_Photographs_of_American_Military_Activity,_1754-1954_Record_Group_111;_National_Archives.

soldiers w/ rifles: http://olive-drab.com/od_other_firearms_rifle_m1917enfield.php

Sgt. York being congratulated: http://www.old-picture.com/american-legacy/011/Sergeant-Alvin-York-C.htm

Self-Control

Chicago & North Western Railway: https://commons.wikimedia.org/wiki/File:Chicago_%26_North_Western_Railway_viaduct_over_Des_Moines_River,_near_Boone,_Iowa_(cropped).jpg

Kate Shelley-teen: https://commons.wikimedia.org/wiki/File:Katherine_Carroll_Shelly.jpg

Thoroughness

Booker T. Washington: Public Domain. http://en.wikipedia.org/wiki/File:Booker_T_Washington_retouched_flattened-crop.jpg

About the Authors

Marilyn Boyer is the mother of fourteen children, all home schooled from kindergarten through high school. Her passion to train up her children in the character of Christ led her to create Character Concepts Curriculum, a character curriculum for kids of all ages to equip parents in raising children of integrity!

Her many character resources, as well as books on homeschooling and Christian parenting, are available online.

About the Authors

Grace Tumas Ehrman holds a degree in history from Liberty University. Her paper, "Warlords and Samurais: Japanese Interventionists in Siberia During the Russian Civil War, 1918-1922," won an award at the 2013 Phi Alpha Theta History Conference. She specializes in American and Russian history.